Memories of M

A Sheffield Interme
1924–1964

Mary M. Bramhill

OBNIXI NON CEDERE

Unite we now Marlcliffians in song our voices raise
Let Marlcliffe's name beloved inspire our joyous lay
Where'er we are or may be in these later years
Marlcliffians yea Marlcliffians we'll proudly be for aye.

Obnixi Non Cedere let this inspire us still
Ne'er yielding in the struggle stern that good may conquer ill
We'll all strive for victory again and yet again
Thus may we Marlcliffe's honour through every age maintain.

Our work at school Marlcliffians we'll tackle with such zest
That joy in books and learning shall every day increase
And knowledge bring the wisdom which guides in life's hard quest
Marlcliffians hence Marlcliffians our efforts must not cease.

Obnixi Non Cedere let this inspire us still
Ne'er yielding in the struggle stern that good may conquer ill
We'll all strive for victory again and yet again
Thus may we Marlcliffe's honour through every age maintain.

To play the game Marlcliffians we will put forth our might
When on the field our mettle is oft times sorely tried
E'en if no victory's wrested from foes in hard fought fight
Marlcliffians we Marlcliffians will yet have cause for pride.

Throughout the years Marlcliffians when days at school are o'er
The spirit that inspires us shall be to all revealed
For those with whom we labour shall know for evermore
Marlcliffians yea Marlcliffians have hearts set not to yield.

Obnixi Non Cedere let this inspire us still
Ne'er yielding in the struggle stern that good may conquer ill
We'll all strive for victory again and yet again
Thus may we Marlcliffe's honour through every age maintain.

Memories of Marlcliffe

A Sheffield Intermediate School
1924–1964

Mary M. Bramhill

1998

© 1998 Mary M. Bramhill

Published by Mary M. Bramhill

Designed and typeset by Interleaf Productions Limited
Printed by the Cromwell Press, Trowbridge, Wiltshire.

All rights reserved. No part of this publication may be reproduced, stored in a retrieval system, or transmitted, in any form or by any means, electronic, mechanical, photocopying, recording or otherwise, without the prior permission in writing of the publishers.

British Library Cataloguing in Publication Data
   Memories of Marlcliffe: a Sheffield intermediate school,
   1924 - 1964
   1. Marlcliffe School   2. Schools - England - Sheffield -
   History - 20th century
   I. Title
   371'.00942821

ISBN 0 9533111 0 4

Contents

	Foreword	7
	Acknowledgements	8
1	The School and its Buildings	9
2	Lessons and Out-of-School Activities	15
3	Wartime	33
4	Pranks and Punishments	39
5	Special Events and Special Care	45
6	The Old Marlcliffians' Association	57

Marlcliffe Intermediate School

Foreword

My congratulations to everyone who has made this book possible, but particularly to Mary Bramhill who not only had the idea of recollecting the history of Marlcliffe Intermediate School but also had the 'get up and go' to do something about it.

I have a very special interest in Marlcliffe Intermediate School because my own sister, Doreen, attended there. Like so many others at the time, she did so because, although bright and able, income, background or family expectation meant that she was unable to take up one of the limited number of places then available for grammar school pupils in Sheffield.

It will be 75 years next year from the time, in 1924, when the City Council decided to experiment with 'intermediate schools'. As spelt out in this short history, that was an adventurous step in developing much greater flexibility in secondary schooling and in providing a rounded and broad experience for youngsters who would otherwise have had an extremely limited chance of gaining a secondary education.

It is by rejoicing in the drive, commitment and vision of others that we can build today an education system of which we can be proud. Those who gave their all, as Mary and many like her have done, are the example we need to build on when we try to re-enthuse our education service with the belief that opportunity should be available to all our children and that we can achieve it.

That is what I am trying to do as Secretary of State for Education and Employment—in transforming the life chances of our children, and putting literacy and numeracy at the very core of the foundation for later lifelong learning and the joy of reading and discovering.

I am grateful to the Mary Bramhills of this world and for this insight into a piece of Sheffield history and the work of Marlcliffe Intermediate School.

David Blunkett 1998
Secretary of State for Education and Employment
MP for Sheffield Brightside

Acknowledgements

Thanks are due to the staff of Sheffield City Archives and the Local Studies Library for their assistance, to Sheffield's Director of Education for permission to quote from the School's Log Books, to the Controller of Her Majesty's Stationery Office for permission to quote from the HMI report on the school, 1952 (Crown Copyright Reference SM 83'52) and to Sheffield Newspapers Limited for allowing me to use the interview printed in the *Sheffield Telegraph* on Miss Nuttall's retirement.

Finally, heartfelt thanks to the numerous former pupils who have made this book possible by sending in their memories, lending photographs and other memorabilia, and answering innumerable questions. Special thanks to Frank Kent for photographing the buildings, to Jane Jordan for typing the manuscript, to Joe Scarborough for the cover design, and to Roy Bullen for help and encouragement in so many ways: these, too, are former pupils.

Chapter One

The School and its Buildings

In 1924, Sheffield Education Committee agreed to make provision for the establishment of schools of a type intermediate between the Elementary and Secondary School: in the words of its report 'to provide a course of instruction more advanced in character and wider in content than that given in the ordinary Elementary School'. At this time, Sheffield compared badly with a number of other large towns in the number of Secondary School places available: in 1923 three hundred children who qualified for entry had to be refused because there were not enough places. In those years of financial stringency, there was no possibility of new buildings being erected, so the original Council Schools at Marlcliffe Road and Greystones Road, which were not being used to capacity, were converted into Intermediates (although part of the Marlcliffe building still housed Juniors and Infants). Two further schools of this type were opened later, Carfield, in 1925, and Owler Lane, in 1926. In the words of a later HMI report on Marlcliffe 'the main purpose of these schools is to provide for those children who, whilst incapable of reaching in the selection tests the standard demanded of Grammar School entrants, are considered by the Authority to be capable of profiting from a more advanced secondary education than can be provided in the Secondary Modern schools'.

Many former pupils would query this description of them as 'incapable of reaching in the selection tests the standard demanded of Grammar School entrants'. Certainly their School Certificate results belied this description and, in a few years, some pupils were naming Marlcliffe rather than one of the Grammar Schools as their first choice if they passed the 11+ examination. This was partly because of the good reputation it enjoyed—as one father said 'If she's any brains they'll come out at Marlcliffe as well as anywhere else!'—but also because there was then no Grammar School on the north side of the city. Parents thought that, if their child could be at a school near home and still take the same School Certificate examination as at a distant Grammar School, why incur the expense and the extra travelling time for their son or daughter?

Moreover, the fact that books were free and the school uniform simple and not too costly was often quite a consideration. One girl remembers starting school at Marlcliffe with a gymslip made from one of her grandmother's navy serge coats, and blouses which were shirts passed down from an elder brother. Another says, 'My mother must have spent hours tacking the pleats of my gymslip before she washed it: dry cleaning was too expensive and 'permanent pleats' hadn't been thought of'.

One old boy, who rose to be a Flight Lieutenant in the Air Force, later wrote: 'In 1924 Sheffield Council took the unprecedented step of introducing free Secondary Schools for boys and girls from impecunious families unable to pay the fees of King Edward's Grammar School and the 'Red Knob's' School at Firth Park, etc.'.

Interestingly, in 1946, the Headmistress of Marlcliffe sent a report to the Education Office suggesting that there might be a wide margin of error in IQ assessment—in other words, the result of the 11+ examination by which pupils passed to Grammar or Intermediate Schools—and that factors other than this were important for academic progress. She mentioned two pupils who failed their School Certificate examination in spite of having IQs of 124 and 121 respectively, whilst ten of the successful candidates had IQs of 113 or less. (She also showed that she considered other things than academic progress important, by mentioning that one of these became Senior Prefect, School Cricket Captain, a House Captain, chief character in the School Play and also won the 'Best Marlcliffian' prize.)

Although, from 1928, Marlcliffe pupils took the same School Certificate examination as those at Grammar Schools, there were other important differences between the two types of school. Entrants to Grammar Schools had to sign to stay for four years and take the examinations, whereas, at an Intermediate School, one could leave at fourteen. In the early days some did leave at fourteen, not through lack of ability but because their parents badly needed the meagre wages that their offspring might earn. In 1929 the Marlcliffe Headmaster tried, by circulars and personal interviews, to persuade parents to let their children stay for the full four years but, as the Education Committee Minutes report, 'many exercised their right to withdraw them when a suitable situation offered'.

If Marlcliffians wanted to go on to take the Higher School Certificate, they then had to move to a Grammar School. At least they would then get travelling expenses: some pupils at Marlcliffe remember walking quite long distances to save the ha'penny tram-fare. One other

The School and its Buildings

difference between the schools that pupils would not know about was that their teachers were paid at the rate for Elementary Schools, even though a number of them had university degrees. In those days a university degree entitled one to teach at a Grammar School and receive a better salary than teachers from a Training College where the course was shorter and geared to providing staff for Elementary Schools. It surely says something for the atmosphere of the school that a number of these highly-qualified teachers were happy to stay on at Marlcliffe for all their teaching career, rather than try to move to a Grammar School.

The school had been built in 1915 on an awkward sloping site, so that the arrangement of classrooms was somewhat unusual (not to say inconvenient). In the semi-basement were the Domestic Science Room, the Science Laboratory and the Stock Room. Owing to the slope, the windows of the Domestic Science Room were almost on a level with the playground, and one Domestic Science teacher remembers a football coming through a window and sprinkling one pupil's soup with glass.

The main floor was used by the Infants and Junior Schools, except for one room used by Intermediate pupils. Staircases at each end of the building (one for boys and one for girls) led up to the top floor, and half-way up were the staff-rooms and the Head's office. At the top of the stairs, swing doors opened onto the pupils' cloakrooms, with handbasins and a large recess for hanging coats. (No lavatories here—those were in the school yard.)

Main Building

New hall

Miss Saunders and Mr Anderson in the temporary classroom in the upstairs hall of the main building

The main part of the school was all on the top floor: nine classrooms opened off a long passage, and the two centre ones faced a large rectangular space which housed a modest library, with books both for loan and reference. Here also were the Head's and the school clerk's desks, the Head's tall one with its high chair standing on a raised platform. By sliding back the glazed partitions of the two centre classrooms, this area was enlarged to provide room for the morning religious assemblies which were always an important part of the school day. Near the Overton Road entrance to the girls' yard stood the caretaker's house. Behind this were what one pupil from the early '30s describes as 'two wooden shacks, one the dining room and the other the woodworking shop'.

Many years later, writing on the occasion of the Headmistress's retirement, another former pupil said '...she has been the life of Marlcliffe from the first day... she ate sandwiches at mid-day, like many others of us, before there was any dining-hall or kitchen, and she ate the first cooked meal with us in the first dining-hall (half an army hut, the other half being the Woodwork Centre)'.

Social conditions in Sheffield at that time were so bad that centres were provided in different areas where needy pupils could get free breakfasts and teas. Since Marlcliffe pupils came from many different parts of the city, some would inevitably be late for morning school because of the distance they had to travel after attending a breakfast centre.

With a fresh intake of pupils each year, it soon became obvious that more accommodation was needed and so a large wooden building was erected. This managed to house not only a kitchen and a dining room but also two classrooms, one of which was used for woodwork and such other activities as printing the school magazine. Also, there were two cycle sheds, as well as the somewhat primitive toilets in the boys' and girls' yards.

However, by early 1937, a grand new building was opened, comprising a spacious assembly hall with a large raised platform, which became the stage for innumerable play productions, a large kitchen and dining room and another staff-room; and, on one side of the hall, at a lower level were three new classrooms. One for what the Chief Education Officer called 'Manual Instruction' (that is, Woodwork), one an Art Room, and one a Science Demonstration Room. Fortunately the girls' yard was sufficiently extensive still to leave room for netball and rounders' practice in the dinner hour—the boys' yard was unaffected.

Two years later came the outbreak of war, and by then the area for recreation in the girls' yard was further reduced by the erection of air-raid shelters. One girl who started at Marlcliffe in 1940 says, 'One of the first things we had to do was air-raid shelter drill'. She remembers the long wooden benches and the dim lights, and goes on, 'It was probably the close confines of the shelters that allowed someone to infect dozens of us with scarlet fever—Marlcliffians just about took over Lodge Moor Hospital that autumn!'

After the war, the Head was again noting in the school Log Book, in 1947, that the school was badly overcrowded—one form was having to work in the dining room and another in the small clinic room at the bottom of the boys' staircase. As a temporary measure, part of the old hall upstairs in the main building was partitioned off to form an extra classroom and, in 1949, work was begun on the provision of three extra classrooms off the boys' staircase, although the lowest of these could be given over to the Junior and Infant School 'according to numbers'. Even as late as this, an HMI's report 'strongly deplored the shortage of lavatories and wash bowls' and suggested that the air-raid shelters ought to be adapted.

In spite of all these improvements to the buildings over the years, it is interesting to remember that the desks still had inkwells, which were filled by monitors: fountain pens were coming in, and eventually ball-point pens, but pupils were not allowed to use ball-points for homework as they were considered to be 'bad for one's handwriting'. The final addition to the buildings—which did not happen until 1960—was a fine, purpose-built gymnasium (before that, the annual gymnastic display had been in the hall and, in spite of the limitations that imposed, it must be said that the standard was always very high).

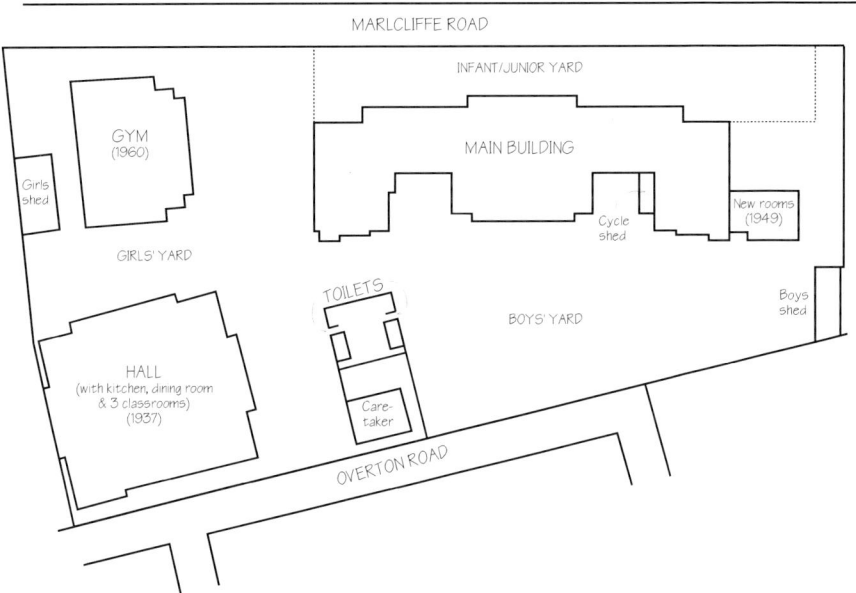

Sketch plan (not to scale)

Chapter Two
Lessons and Out-of-School Activities

So much for the buildings, but it is the staff and pupils who make a school, and I am sure that Old Marlcliffians will agree that it is particularly the staff. Few memories have come in from the earliest pupils, but it is obvious that from the start there was a tremendous and lively spirit, and a wonderful rapport between staff and pupils; all realised that the opening of this new type of school was a great challenge and they were determined to meet it.

When the school opened the Headmaster was Mr Walter E. Smith. One early entrant described him as 'a powerful, persuasive, genteel leader...ably supported by a team of young dedicated enthusiasts'. In Mr Smith's own report on the school in 1929 he says:

> *I desire to point out, respectfully but most emphatically, that our successes do not arise from a system of 'cramming'; they are the natural consequence of concentration from a wide and generous curriculum, combined with a system of important school activities generously and conscientiously developed.*

Amongst his staff of seven was Miss Nellie Nuttall BA, teaching English, who followed him as Head when he moved on to become a School Inspector in 1930.

Incidentally, Miss Nuttall was promoted to the Headship without the post being advertised 'an appointment sufficiently rare to merit more than passing notice' according to a later HMI's report.

On Mr Smith's leaving, Miss Nuttall described him as 'inspiring and undaunted...one who taught the value and the joy of work' and 'for scholars living under hard conditions at home he had both understanding and help'. The attitude of staff and pupils obviously paid off, as one girl who attended during the first four years 'cannot remember that anyone failed School Certificate'. In fact, records show that in 1928, out of 21 candidates, seven gained their School Certificate and thirteen the higher qualification of Matriculation. Quite early on, the House system was established. At first, there were four Houses but this was changed in 1936 to three—Ewden, Loxley and Rivelin (the names of the three rivers which flow into the River Don). Inter-House rivalry, particularly in sports, made for much enthusiasm.

Most of the Old Marlcliffians who contributed their memories mentioned the staff who taught during their schooldays but, in quoting from them, I shall not give any names, excepting those of the first Headmaster, Mr Walter Smith; Miss Nuttall, Headmistress for 32 years; and also the long-serving Senior Master and Senior Mistress. However, here are some of the Old Marcliffian's comments, and former pupils amongst the readers can amuse themselves by deciding to which member of staff each refers:

> *…who taught PT and walked about with green knickers showing below her gymslip.*

> *In the words of Miss Nuttall 'the first gentleman in England' who was very kind and polite to all.*

> *I can see him now, illustrating the conversion of Paul on the Damascus Road by pushing the class piano one way and—after the conversion—the other way, across the classroom.*

> *She had the habit of leaning back in her chair, which was not only precarious, but always opened up a gap between her upper and lower garments.*

> *Was well known for sucking her pencil all the time—used to talk with it in her mouth.*

> *My first form mistress—I think she was adored by all.*

> *…who gave me a love of classical music because he always played records as the class filed in for lessons.*

> *…one of my favourites used to recite monologues—for example, 'Albert and the Lion'—he was so funny and very kind.*

She walked so briskly along the corridors, her black gown billowing out behind. She always wore a thin velvet ribbon in her silver-white hair, and lace-up Cuban-heeled shoes...her small brown eyes missed very little.

Yes, this was Miss Nuttall—who soon gave us our wonderful school motto *Obnixi non cedere*—(determined not to yield). She also wrote the school song, which was set to music by Mr W. Fletcher.

So much for the idiosyncrasies of some of the staff. Consider now the school day: first came the daily religious assembly: pupils filed in to music, each clutching the 'Songs of Praise' given out on their first day. There was a hymn, a prayer and a lesson from the Bible, chosen and read by members of the staff in turn. Many remember Miss Nuttall's talks at special times in the Christian year—Easter, Whitsuntide, etc. School notices would be read out and also, during the war, any news of former pupils who were in the Forces. Now for the subjects taught. One of the 1924 entrants to the school lists subjects taken in the first School Certificate examination four years later: English, Mathematics, French, History, Geography, Chemistry (Boys–Physics), Music and Scripture. Apart from these formal examinations, once a year an 'Honorary Examiner in Biblical Knowledge' came round the schools and questioned the pupils. This was not looked forward to, but Marlcliffe always came out well from the ordeal: one examiner reported, 'My visit to this school will remain an inspiring memory...the atmosphere is a tribute to the skill and devotion of Miss Nuttall and her staff'.

The School Log Book, kept by the Head, always recorded the School Certificate results in detail, including the percentage of passes, the number who gained Matriculation, and how the results compared with those of other schools in the city. Already, in 1934, the percentage of passes at Marlcliffe was higher than those of all the other schools examined (and in 1935 and 1937 higher in all but two subjects); and indeed this was a trend that continued more often than not. By now there were more subjects taken: Composition as well as English Literature, Oral French as well as Written, and Art. Even in 1940, 22 out of 28 candidates gained their School Certificate—a result which the Chief Education Officer considered to be 'highly satisfactory, considering the time missed through war conditions'.

Another result of the war—that several male teachers joined the Forces—is shown by the Head's entry in the Log Book for 1941 'There have been many changes of staff, and eight subjects were taken by teachers who had never before taught a School Certificate class: the 80% of passes is therefore highly satisfactory'. Nevertheless, Miss Nuttall's priorities are revealed in this comment from a girl who left in 1941 'Miss Nuttall discovered

The School Song

OBNIXI NON CEDERE

Unite we now Marlcliffians in song our voices raise
Let Marlcliffe's name beloved inspire our joyous lay
Where'er we are or may be in these later years
Marlcliffians yea Marlcliffians we'll proudly be for aye.

Obnixi Non Cedere let this inspire us still
Ne'er yielding in the struggle stern that good may conquer ill
We'll all strive for victory again and yet again
Thus may we Marlcliffe's honour through every age maintain.

Our work at school Marlcliffians we'll tackle with such zest
That joy in books and learning shall every day increase
And knowledge bring the wisdom which guides in life's hard quest
Marlcliffians hence Marlcliffians our efforts must not cease.

Obnixi Non Cedere let this inspire us still
Ne'er yielding in the struggle stern that good may conquer ill
We'll all strive for victory again and yet again
Thus may we Marlcliffe's honour through every age maintain.

To play the game Marlcliffians we will put forth our might
When on the field our mettle is oft times sorely tried
E'en if no victory's wrested from foes in hard fought fight
Marlcliffians we Marlcliffians will yet have cause for pride.

Throughout the years Marlcliffians when days at school are o'er
The spirit that inspires us shall be to all revealed
For those with whom we labour shall know for evermore
Marlcliffians yea Marlcliffians have hearts set not to yield.

Obnixi Non Cedere let this inspire us still
Ne'er yielding in the struggle stern that good may conquer ill
We'll all strive for victory again and yet again
Thus may we Marlcliffe's honour through every age maintain.

to her horror that some of us didn't know the Ten Commandments by heart...we could leave Marlcliffe without sex education or careers guidance but not without knowing the Ten Commandments'.

At this time, some teachers found themselves helping out in subjects for which their training had not really prepared them: for instance, the Art teacher took some third year Essay and first year Music lessons. Here are two brief compositions from those essays, both by girls:

On Walking in the Rain

One!, two!, three!, four!, five!, six!, seven!, eight! The clock on the Town Hall chimed the hour, 8 o'clock am. The city centre which had, since 12 o'clock pm the night before been nearly deserted, was awakened by the loud peals of the bells. People went to shops and unlocked them; some policemen checked the time by their watches and eagerly looked for the next one on that beat; flower women found their particular stands in the markets. Everyone seemed so happy until ten past eight; then it began to rain. Slowly at first, then faster and faster till the ground was very wet. The shopkeepers sighed, 'Oh! Drat the weather. However are we supposed to sell if it is raining and no one comes?'

Early Memories

As I look back over the years of my early childhood and think over my early memories, now that I am much older I am inclined to laugh at them. One thing which made me at the time very pleased with myself was the memorable day when I first tied a bow on my shoes without anyone's assistance. This new discovery made me insist on untying and tying my shoes, my mother's apron strings, my own hair ribbon and anything which was convenient at the time. Another memorable occasion was the day when I learnt how to write and spell my own name. This new knowledge gave me great satisfaction.

An account of the last Speech Day before the war broke out shows an ambitious programme. First, all stood to sing the National Anthem, then came part-songs, followed by a speech by the Chairman, Alderman Harold Jackson LLB. (Alderman—later Sir—Harold Jackson was always a great friend and supporter of the school.) This was followed by the Head Teacher's Annual Report. After that, more songs, and then an address and the all-

1935
Mr Tomlinson, Mr Kelsey, Miss Jackson
Mr Swindell, Miss Coatsworth, Mr Beynon, Mr Scowcroft, Mr Egerton, Miss Varah
Miss Renshaw, Mr Reynolds, Miss Nuttall, Miss Hawkins, Mr Parkin

Display in Art Room 1953–54

Lessons and Out-of-School Activities

important distribution of certificates and prizes by Sir Louis Smith MP. A vote of thanks to Sir Louis followed, then more songs, a vote of thanks to the Chairman, and finally an appropriate anthem 'How Calmly the Evening' by Sir Edward Elgar. The pupil with the highest number of passes—11, of which 9 were at A level—was also awarded the prize for 'the best Marlcliffian'. The ethos of the school is shown by several prizes not for specific subjects but for such matters as handwriting, perseverance, tidiness in mind and work.

Many more activities went on at Marlcliffe out of school hours. As time went on, the School Magazine recorded the meetings of the Wireless and Scientific Society (it later dropped the 'Wireless' bit of its name), the Ramblers' Society (later there were two groups, Senior and Junior), the Handicraft Guild, a French Circle and a Knitting Circle, and groups for both Folk and Modern Dancing, and even—when there happened to be a teacher adept at the subject—Ballet Dancing. One of Her Majesty's Inspectors later commented, 'the outstanding feature of these meetings is the delightfully informal way in which the boys and girls and members of staff meet together'.

To many the most important of these activities was the Dramatic Society. Every year from 1928 (with the exception of 1940) a play was produced. These ranged from classics such as Sheridan's 'The Rivals' and Shaw's 'Saint Joan' to A.A. Milne's 'Toad of Toad Hall'. For the actors, this entailed staying after school for innumerable rehearsals: one of them

Ballet 'Les Trois Citrons'   May 1947

recalls 'taking sandwiches and a flask of cocoa for tea…and then travelling home late on the tram in the dark. Nevertheless, we were not excused homework!'

For the staff involved in these productions, there was the construction and painting of the scenery, the making of costumes, the collection of all the other items that the set required and the printing of programmes and posters. The production of the play was in the hands of the Senior English Mistress and was always most professional, in fact for some pupils the highlight of their schooldays was taking part in the play. One girl recounts that acting in these productions 'fuelled my desire to pursue acting seriously' and at the age of seventeen she gained her Diploma from the London Guildhall School of Music and Drama and, after the war, became a founder member of one of Sheffield's leading amateur dramatic groups, the Denys Edward Players.

The Senior Ramblers' Society combined all-day Saturday walks with visits to places of interest and occasional Youth Hostel week-ends, not only to such Derbyshire venues as Hartington and Bretton, but also farther afield to Loch Lomond. One boy remembers that his last day at school was followed by a week's walking holiday in the Lake District with

Scene from 'Make Believe' 1959

his form-mates, led by his form teacher and another member of staff; this surely shows the warm relationship between staff and scholars. After the war there were also barbecues, with bacon and sausages on sticks cooked over an open fire (at one of which the members had to learn the useful art of how to put out a brushwood fire, as the surrounding bushes started to flare up). Latterly, the year's activities would end with a treasure hunt. The first clue would be given out at the end of afternoon school, this revealed the starting point, then the hunt took place that evening. Further rhyming clues were given out at the start, such as:

> *You'd like to borrow a book today?*
> *Now which day can't you, tell me pray.*

and

> *There's an old-fashioned pub on the site of something older*
> *You could ask the landlord what, if you're feeling bolder.*

These led to Ecclesall Library and the Smithy Bar of the local inn. The final clue led to the leader's garden, where the prize was given out and the members were refreshed with home-made ginger beer and scones. As with other activities, such as inter-school matches, some unfortunate had the task of writing an account of the outing and reading it out in assembly on the following Monday morning.

Apart from these local excursions, various members of staff arranged visits further afield: to York, Harrogate, Stratford-upon-Avon and even abroad. In 1938 a ten-day visit to Paris cost pupils about £6 and—oh dear!—one boy dropped his return ticket from the top of the Eiffel Tower! In the following year, it had gone up to £8 according to one girl: she recalls 'I couldn't go, as my mum said that would take the whole family to the seaside for a week'. These trips resumed after the war, and by then were becoming more adventurous. Of a visit to Belgium in 1946 one boy wrote 'The first impression we had of Belgium was of neon lights…thousands of them…Blimey! It's in technicolour … In the morning we walked round the shops and I noticed how many beggars there were in the streets. It was pitiable to see men without legs, dressed in desperately ragged clothes, pulling themselves along in little soap-box trucks; and these disabled soldiers, we were told, were the better-off beggars'. In 1949 a party went to Switzerland—'it was magical and Montreux was like a fairy tale'. In 1950 there was a coach tour of Holland and Belgium; the Sheffield United Tours' coach was hoisted on deck by a crane—no drive-on ferries in those days.

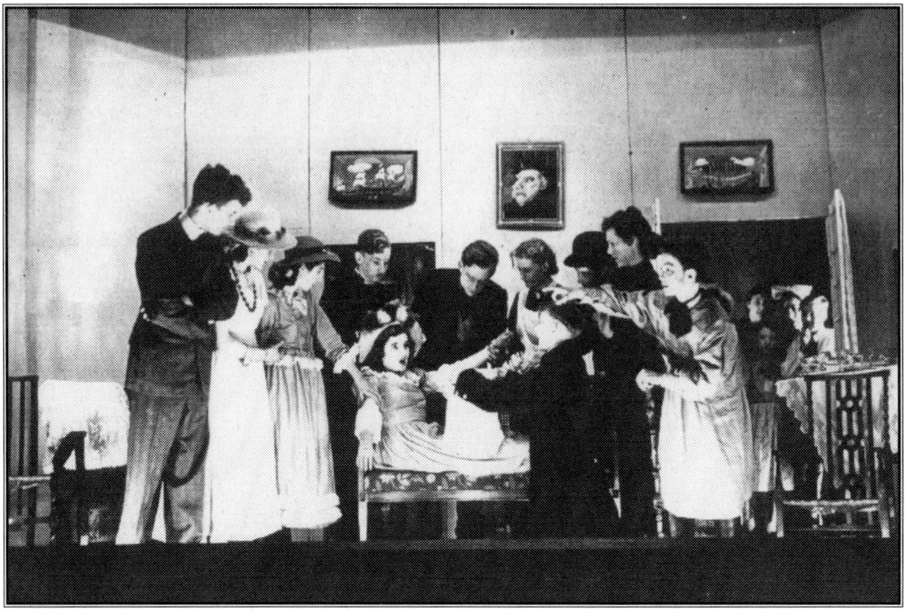

Scene from 'The Farmer's Wife'   1947

Cast of 'Through the Crack'   1945

Senior Ramblers Group   Kinder 1959

Marlcliffe Ramble 1959

A Senior Ramblers Group

School visit to Holland   1950

Barbecue on Stanage Edge, with Miss Nuttall and Mrs Bramhill

All these activities, sports events and Inter-House matches were recorded in the school magazine 'The Marlcliffian'. This was started the very term the school opened, as a double sheet of cyclostyled paper. This was soon a very full twice-yearly production, printed on the School Press in the Woodwork Room. It opened with a short report by the editor (one of the staff) followed by all sorts of articles. In 1934, for example, there were 'Hints on Entering Business', and a letter from a boy who had gone on to Magdalen College, Oxford; then, in 1961, there was a request for wool for the Knitting Circle to enable them to knit blankets for refugees. Various educational visits in the city were also described from time to time, such as a lecture in the City Hall on 'The World of the Atom' and others on such subjects as 'Climbing Mount Everest', 'The Story of the Bible', 'The Civil War in Spain' and 'Old Music'. Outings to the theatre and Hallé concerts are mentioned several times. Incidentally, full school uniform had, of course, to be worn on such occasions, and one boy tells how some of the seniors, having by then lost their school caps, would (temporarily, one hopes) pinch them from the 'fusties' (first-year scholars).

There were occasional poems and even parodies in the magazine, such as the one which started:

A Marlcliffe scholar, may his knowledge increase,
Awoke one night from a deep dream of peace.

Certainly, humour was not lacking: there was an 'editorial cat' who somehow managed to ferret out a number of howlers, such as 'Sheffield Steal is world famous', 'After tea I played a game of chest', 'Caesar was told to beware the hides of March', 'the meaning of bellicose is indigestion' and 'Orpheus took his liar with him'. There were also lino-cut illustrations, the designing and cutting of the blocks done in the Art Room and the printing in the Woodwork Room.

Two, more serious, literary contributions from senior pupils are given here both written in 1961, the first by a girl in 5A and the second by a boy in 5B.

An Empty House

I opened the garden gate and gazed at the ghostly house. The path was paved and sooty, and grass was growing in every crevice; the garden was like a jungle, overgrown and neglected, with weeds springing up like trees, and rambler roses twisting their way into the neighbouring garden; the cold grey stones of the house, and its shattered windows, seemed to give an air of mystery to the place.

As I walked through the door the rusty hinges creaked terrifyingly. Cobwebs were draped everywhere, strings of dust hung like beaded curtains in the doorway and an old zinc bucket, like a lone sentinel, stood on guard over the empty fireplace. My curiosity drew me up the squeaking stairs over a carpet of dust to reach the long-forgotten bedroom where mellow sunlight reappeared at the dirty broken window.

There on the floor an old newspaper, yellow with age, lay amid peelings from the damp walls. A child's doll was tossed carelessly in a corner, pathetically lying with beetles, ants and spiders. The room reeked with a musty, dusty odour: even the iron bars across the lower windows gave out a dry smell of rust that added to the dark and dismal atmosphere. Dusk was gradually creeping from the room, leaving shadows lurking behind the decaying doors. The house seemed miserable and cheerless, completely forgotten in a row of gay houses. It made me wonder what the house was like before it was deserted by the inhabitants. I could imagine the Christmas festivities, the laughter of bygone days: happy memories for someone now caught in a tangle of ruin and despair.

As I came out of the house, twilight was beginning to fall, and dew was settling on the unkempt hedge and rusty iron gate, increasing my feeling of desolation.

The Old Boat

*At the end of the wharf lies a strange old hulk
Rotted beyond repair.
From the midst of the sails the cabins sulk
And the vacant portholes stare.*

*The slime-covered deck with weeds bestrewn
Has not been trod for years,
But the boards creak out a woeful tune
And the ragged weeds shed tears.*

*The sodden sail hangs as a shroud,
Ridiculous in its pride
But the dockyard cats protest aloud
As down the deck they slide.*

*Creaking spars and oozing beams,
Twisted bulwark leaking,
Water squeezing through the seams
And rusted pulleys squeaking.*

*Patches of oil flow round the bows
Rudder groans in pain,
A groaning like a herd of cows;
Pain recedes again.*

*Pensioned off from active life
You have tarried long,
Is it not time to quit your strife
And end your twisted song?*

THE MARLCLIFFIAN

No. 41   19th printed at Marlcliffe   December, 1953

Lino cut illustrations for the School Magazine

Memories of Scotland

Lessons and Out-of-School Activities

The subjects taken in the school, and the excellent results in the School Certificate Examination, have already been mentioned, but a little more detail as to what the lessons were actually like would fill out the picture.

Fortunately, at least one boy has kept, and made available, two of his rough notebooks and a composition book from his first two years at Marlcliffe. So, here is an example of English homework: 'Make up two sentences containing proper and common nouns, two containing abstract nouns, one sentence with a noun in the nominative case, one in the accusative, one in the genitive and one in the vocative'. The age of this pupil? Eleven! In Algebra, given that $a = 3$, $b = 2$, $c = 1$, $x = 4$, $y = 10$, $z = 5$, find the value of, for instance, $5 \times ab$ and $6b \div x$. In French, he was expected to be able to say not only 'Open the door' but also such useful sentences as 'No, it is not the girl, it is the boy'. In Science, he had to explain how to find the weight of 1cc of water or, more usefully, why the sea keeps a fairly constant level in spite of the vast amount of water added by the rivers. In the following year he manages to spell such words as: fascinating, encyclopaedia, irreconcilable and iridescent correctly, only falling down on such as incorrigible and reciprocity. One wonders whether he could still 'list in order the ministers, etc. of Charles II's reign' as he was required to do in his history homework. Essay subjects ranged from such imaginative ones as 'A Stormy Sea' to the practical 'Reply to an advertisement in the paper for an apprentice printer'.

Incidentally, homework meant three subjects a night (with one free night a week) and a pupil was expected to spend an hour on each. Also, to learn twenty lines of poetry a week—as one girl comments 'I am ever grateful for this'.

In 1950 one teacher collected some of the pupils' work in a 'Book of Third Year Essays' where are found such subjects as 'The Most Deplorable Invention of the Past Century' (this was the tram!) 'The Imaginary Autobiography of an Ordinary Woman', and 'Britain Today and a Hundred Years Ago'.

Happily, the same boy who struggled with such difficult homework in his first year also enjoyed all the school's sports activities: he records cricket and football matches against the other three Intermediate Schools (Greystones, Carfield and Owler Lane) and also against the Junior Technical School—'we play like hell!'—the Roman Catholic De La Salle School and High Storrs Grammar School. Another boy records his heart-felt appreciation of the Head who gave the school a half-day holiday to watch Sheffield Wednesday play Preston North End in a mid-week Cup-Tie.

One innovation that should be mentioned was the introduction, in 1944, of an extra class of 40 pupils who had decided, at the age of 13, that they would like to become teachers. They were put in the charge of the Senior English Mistress and, since they could hardly be called '3D' (there were already forms 3A, B and C) she hit on the inspiring name of 'Pioneers'. She introduced them to great thinkers, writers, historical characters, artists and musicians by means of a fascinating book which had recently been published called 'Van Loon's Lives'.

Another similar class came in the following year but, as no one could think of a special name for these pupils, they were called 'Intending Teachers', soon abbreviated to ITs. There are no statistics to confirm how many of these late entrants actually became teachers but certainly one girl was later Head of an Infants' School in the city.

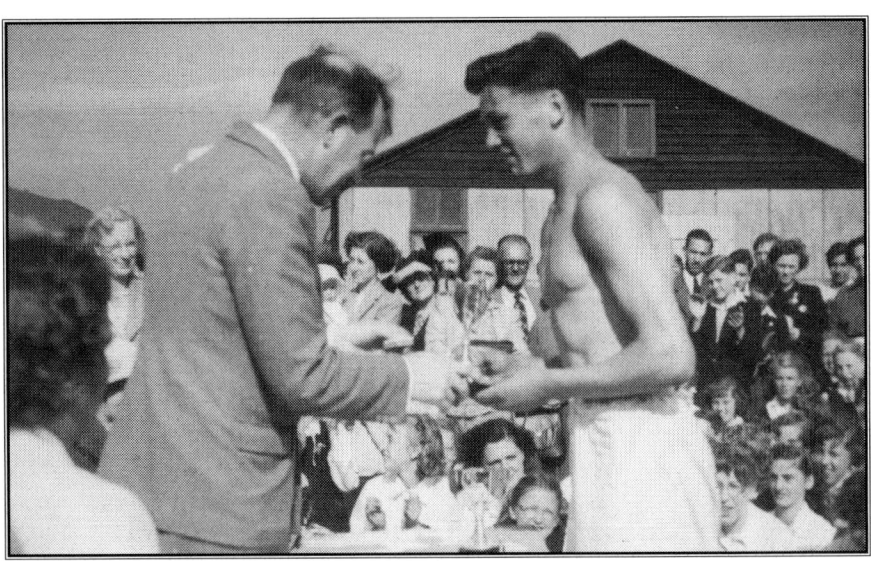

Cup Presentation   Sports Day 1951

Chapter Three
Wartime

Many pupils who were at school during World War II have mentioned air-raid practices. One remembers that at one end of the shelters there were shelves stacked with chocolate bars; as the pupils were never in the shelters long enough for these to be given out, she wonders what happened to this chocolate. (Could there be a connection here with the master one boy remembers as sometimes eating a bar of chocolate during lessons? Perish the thought!) As early as 1938 the Art Room and Science Demonstration Room had been used for the fitting and distribution of gas masks and, in the following year, teachers were recalled early from the summer holidays to help with preparation for the evacuation of children from the city.

Sheffield parents were, however, reluctant to send their children away so, until air-raid shelters could be provided, the schools were closed and what was known as 'Home Service' began. In September 1939 Marlcliffe staff visited the homes of all scholars to make arrangements for this; groups of not more than 12 were to have lessons in a home within a few minutes' walk of where they lived. Considering the number of pupils, it is not surprising that this took two weeks. The Head decided that sessions should start with prayers and a short scripture reading and, as well as subject-lessons, some time could be given to community singing or a game.

Homework had still to be done but, on the whole, the scholars enjoyed this new experience. What the staff felt is not recorded but they cannot have found it very satisfactory and probably didn't care for all the extra walking involved. School dinners, which had started in the early Thirties at fivepence (then went up to sixpence) had to be discontinued. Fortunately this state of affairs did not last too long and it is recorded in the School

Log Book that the school re-opened full time on April 1st 1940, with temporary air-raid shelters having been made by stacking up sandbags against the low windows of the Science Laboratory.

School dinners were available a week later, although the price had gone up to eightpence. Several comments on school dinners have come in—not surprisingly, perhaps, all from girls. Even in wartime, things were very civilised, proper tablecloths and jugs of water were on the tables. The food generally seems to have been appreciated, though not the fact that nothing must be left on one's plate without permission from the teacher on duty. One boy secreted his unwanted portion of cabbage in his blazer pocket! As a girl recounts 'Miss Nuttall would brook no wastage, on two counts: firstly, wasting food in wartime was not to be borne and, secondly, the cook's efforts were not to be slighted'. Yet another pupil remembers that the staff, at their table on the platform in the hall, had chips—a delicacy never enjoyed by the pupils in those days. If you simply did not like, or could not afford, school dinners, you could bring a packed lunch, and by this time two or three tables were set aside for this.

Nevertheless, although the school was on full time again, things were not by any means back to normal: on May 2nd 1940 came a notice from the Education Office stating that schools should be closed on Wednesday afternoons and open on Saturday mornings 'to ensure that any emergency evacuation plans can be operated immediately'. (Three days later they had second thoughts about this and ruled out the Saturday morning opening.)

By the end of June it was decided that, if there had been an air-raid warning overnight, school hours should be 11.00 am to 4.00 pm: and by September 4th there had been so many alarms that these restricted hours were to be permanent—only to be changed on September 30th to 10.00 am to 4.00 pm, with the proviso that 'closing time can be modified if thought necessary'.

At Marlcliffe, lessons were made shorter, and the mid-morning break cut out. By December the various societies which normally met in the evenings were allowed, because of the black-out and the possibility of air-raids, to have their activities in the afternoon. However, no sooner had this been decided than the first, and very heavy, air-raid came, on the night of December 12th–13th. Next day there were no trams or buses, so only 87 brave scholars made it to school. (It should be recorded that one of the female staff walked seven miles!) No lessons that day, but games, carol singing and even a party of sorts in the afternoon.

After another raid two nights later, schools were closed and all teachers were called upon to help at Rest Centres or in billeting. Eventually, after a longer-than-usual Christmas holiday, schools were re-opened on January 20th 1941, and the very next day came the first air-raid alert during school hours. The Log Book reports 'since scholars going through town have great difficulty over transport because of crowds of workers travelling home about 4.30 pm the time-table was altered to allow them to leave school at 3.45 pm'. Also, two days later, the Director of Education decided that schools should open later, at 9.45 am, again because of transport problems.

Indeed, difficulties in getting to school are mentioned by a number of former pupils. Even before the war one enterprising group of boys skated to school on frosty mornings, using 'split garden canes which we sandpapered smooth—one cane under each foot made an excellent skate at cheap cost'. In the summer they used roller-skates but the Head soon became aware of this and ordered that skates were not to be brought into school. The group overcame this little difficulty by leaving their skates under a hedge in a nearby road and collecting them at home time.

Other more poignant details emerge: one boy's diary tells of going to live with an aunt until his own home was repaired after the big raid. And even five months later he still records 'sirens went three times and some guns...guns again at night...raid—plane down at Heeley'.

Other results of wartime difficulties have been recorded, such as having the annual Sports Day in the school yard because there were no air-raid shelters up at the playing fields at Myers Grove Lane. Indeed, it was not until 1945 that full Sports Days at the field were resumed and, by then, there was a bus provided, cutting out the long walk to beyond Malin Bridge, (variously described as taking anything up to an hour).

In the production of plays, considerable ingenuity was required to overcome some of the difficulties during the war years. The Woodwork Department could not obtain the usual supplies; material for making costumes was 'on coupons'[1], so a great deal of re-cycling and other expedients were resorted to—one of the cast of 'Saint Joan' remembers knitting the armour in string, after which it was somehow painted silver! Some costumes were adapted from borrowed ones—one member of staff even lent her wedding dress. As it was wartime, this was not the conventional long white affair, but a two-piece in corded silk. The background scenery was painted on linen-covered flats which were washed clean after each production but obviously they would not last for ever and at this time the only sufficiently-strong material which was 'off coupons' was tailor's canvas, only made in 18 inch width. So, one year, the Needlework Department had the laborious task of joining up lengths of this to make the necessary width to re-cover the flats.

---

1. Coupons were a means of restriction on the buying of consumable materials during World War II and for some time afterwards.

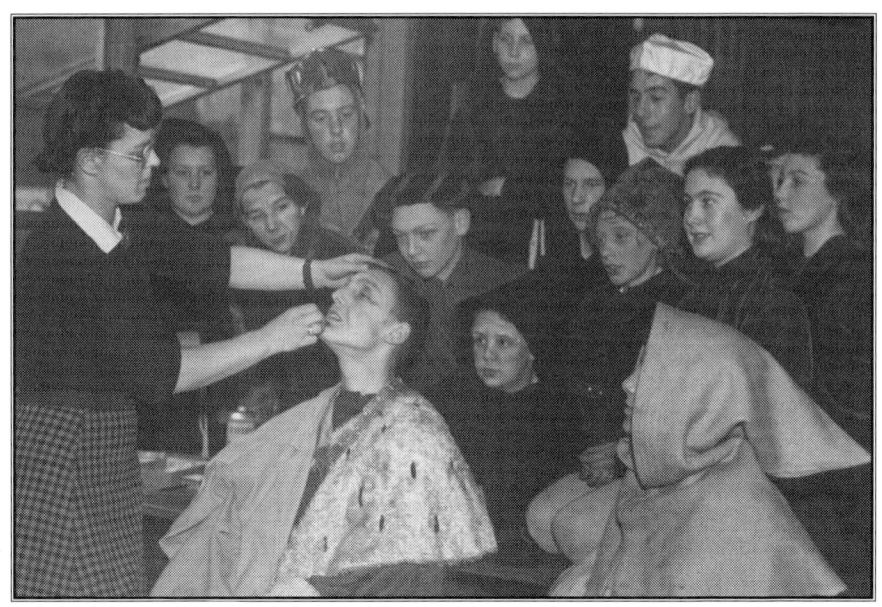

Miss Gallimore making-up the cast of 'St Joan' 1944

Cast of 'Lady With a Lamp' 1943

On the credit side, one girl remembers her parents being given extra clothing coupons to buy her school uniform but she also tells that, because of rationing, the girls had to provide their own ingredients for cookery lessons—these included powdered egg and dried milk. The very limited amount of meat available perhaps accounts for another girl particularly remembering cheese and potato pie and stuffed potatoes. Domestic Science, as it used to be called, also included washing and ironing: the flat irons would be heated on the large gas range and then rubbed on sandstone to make them slide more easily over the clothes. Cookery caps and aprons were made in the Needlework Class; one pupil remembers girls designing their own monograms in the Art Room which were then embroidered on their caps and aprons in Needlework lessons. Another tells of making PE shorts out of blackout material—and hating having to wear them! (This cloth was used to darken house windows: air-raid wardens patrolled the streets at night to see that no chinks of light showed through which could guide enemy planes.)

The Headmistress's own contribution was towards paper-saving: two extra lines were to be ruled at the top and bottom of each page in exercise books, and no new books were given out until old ones were produced, completely filled. Considering the number of pupils, and the number of exercise books used (one at least for each subject), this must have made a considerable saving.

One more activity, in which at least a small party of Marlcliffians became involved, should perhaps be mentioned. In spite of the work of the Women's Land Army, farmers were still very short of help at harvest times and so, in the Autumn of 1945, (and again in the following year) a dozen or so of the older girls and two of the women teachers volunteered to go potato-picking for a week at a War Agricultural Camp. They were based in the village hall of Rawcliffe, near Goole. Well over fifty years later, the conditions these pupils endured seem amazing. They slept on two-tiered bunks, and on arrival had to fill their own pillowcases with straw! There was, of course, no bathroom—they shared three sinks and one toilet. They had to bring their own mug, plate, dish and cutlery (labelled with their name) and each morning they travelled to the fields sitting on the hard floor of a trailer pulled by the farmer's tractor. The farmer provided mid-morning and mid-afternoon drinks, and sandwiches at lunch-time. Meanwhile, the two teachers (quite unqualified in cookery—one taught Art and the other French) struggled with preparations for a substantial evening meal. In the evenings it was usually chattering or playing cards; but there was an Army camp nearby and one day the officer-in-charge came and mentioned, somewhat diffidently, that normally his men had a dance in the Village Hall on a Friday evening and would the Marlcliffe party mind if they continued this practice? After being assured that the behaviour of his men towards the schoolgirls would be impeccable, the staff agreed to this. Needless to say, the girls thought it was marvellous—the appeal of a uniform was very strong in those days.

1947

Mr Anderson, Miss Gallimore, Mr Bainbridge, Mr Curtis, Miss Gregory, Mr Harrington,
Mr Thompson, Mrs Scowcroft, Mr Booth
Mrs Swift, Miss Mattocks, Mr Reynolds, Miss Nuttall, MissCoatsworth, Mr Parkin, Mr Hunt
Miss Wiley   Miss Green

All eyes on the cup as Sir Harold Jackson presents the Jackson Trophy to the winning houses at Marlcliffe School

Chapter Four
Pranks and Punishments

Although, from the start, Marlcliffe was a tight-knit community, it was not by any means cut off from the world outside. The Headmistress frequently spoke of duty to one's neighbours and this was expressed in various ways. Every year there was a special Harvest Festival Service: in 1934 flowers and fruit were sent to the Royal Infirmary and the Children's Hospital; later King Edward VII Hospital was included, and gifts would also be sent to any past and present scholars who were ill. The Log Book reports that in 1940 'the school made a very special effort, with posters, House Competitions, etc. for Sheffield War Weapons' Week, and National Savings Certificates and Stamps sold in this week amounted to £339 15s'. Consideration for one's immediate neighbours was not forgotten: local people were not to be pestered by pupils asking to retrieve lost balls from their gardens—if you kicked a ball into someone's garden, then you had lost it for good. As one boy remarks 'Miss Nuttall was proud of her school, and was most scathing at assembly if she had heard of any incident which reflected on the good name of the school—for example, noisy behaviour on the tramcar or in the street, eating chips (from the shop at the bottom of Darwin Road) in the street'.

Sports Days and Prize Givings brought rewards, both personal and for one's House; but obviously Marlcliffians were not saints, so there had to be punishments as well (although one of the earliest pupils says 'We never saw any canes or met any threats—just exemplary leadership of immaculate behaviour': halcyon days!) So there were lines, detentions, and for really serious misdemeanours—and then only for boys—the cane. Even prefects could give lines—after all, they were responsible for order on the staircases—but that does not seem to have happened very often. If the staff gave lines as a punishment, they decided what the culprit must write. One boy remembers being given the line 'It is inconceivable that I should imagine I could escape punishment for such unco-operative behaviour!' Another enterprising lad decided that he could augment his meagre pocket money by writing lines for fellow sufferers and selling them. Others found that one could get through the task more quickly by writing down instead of across the page, that is, 'I, I, I' 50 (or 100) times, then 'must, must, must', then 'not, not, not', etc. Detentions meant staying in after school and writing a set essay. Punctuality was considered very important, so there were detentions for being late for school, and bad weather—even snow—was no excuse (a sensible pupil would have set off earlier). However, on at least one occasion, the teacher on detention-duty excused all those whose late arrival had been because of traffic hold-ups in the heavy snow—even though the detentions had been given by the Headmistress!

One boy thought he was on to a good thing when he discovered that the subject given for essay homework was the same as his sister had been given six years earlier and, since she had kept her school books, he only had to copy it. Alas, he was found out and 'all I got was a clip round the ear and the advice to stick to Maths and Science'. This same boy later won the Art Prize; but not for drawing a cartoon of the Music Master in the dust on the wall over a radiator—it was the cane for that.

The storage of an emergency cache of chocolate in the air-raid shelters has already been mentioned, but apparently some was kept in the Handicraft cupboard as well and, on one occasion, this was stolen. Not only were the culprits caned but their parents were interviewed and both parents and pupils were urged to build up the store of chocolate again.

On another occasion the school was having a music rehearsal for Speech Day: at a dramatic moment in a piece from 'Judas Maccabeus', where the cry goes up 'Sound an Alarm!', one humorist blew a loud whistle—this resulted in an apoplectic Music Master and the administration of the cane. Incidentally, he comments 'I must say that in this day and age of so-called sophisticated punishment, the stick did us no harm at all'.

The generally free-and-easy attitude to the staff is shown well by a 4C boy's ode (a parody) to one of the staff (who left Marlcliffe in July 1961):

Ode to Mr Williams

Steve he's in his hammock and twelve thousand miles away
Captain are you sleeping there below?
Slung between the palm trees in Opotiki Bay
And dreaming all the time of Marlcliffe, O!
Yonder looms the sports field, yonder lie the teams,
With football players kicking, heel and toe,
The floodlights flashing, and the grey rain splashing,
He sees it all so plainly as he saw it long ago.

Steve he was a Welshman, and ruled the Rugby field.
Captain art thou sleeping there below?
Roving though his boat sailed, he went with heart at ease,
And dreaming all the time of Marlcliffe, O!
'Take my boots to England, hang them by the posts,
Use them when your spirit's running low'.
If King Edward's tip the scales, he'll quit the Maori trail
And we'll chase them off the goal line, as we chased them long ago.

Steve he's in New Zealand, till the three long years he's done.
Captain are you sleeping there below?
Slung between the blackboards, a sleeping in the sun,
And dreaming all the time of Marlcliffe, O!
Call him on the deep sea, call him on the sound,
Call him when we go to meet the foe;
Where his old tricks he's trying and his Welsh flag he's flying,
We shall find him 'ware and waking as we found him long ago.

After one Christmas concert somebody plugged a sink in the boys' cloakroom, causing a flood. The punishment for this was simple—nobody allowed home until the perpetrator confessed. Obviously there were other pranks never found out by teachers: 'fusties' (that is, first-year pupils) would sometimes have their heads pushed into the toilets and 'flushed'. If you happened to be wearing your prized school cap, this was just too bad.

Although there was great enthusiasm for games, not everybody enjoyed them, and one boy remembers evading football by hiding behind the pavilion at Myers Grove playing fields. This same pupil, being creative (he later became an Art Teacher and Lecturer) made water bombs out of paper and lobbed them out of an upstairs window, narrowly missing the member of staff on play-time duty in the yard. Another was so often 'out for a duck' at cricket that he was dubbed 'one-ball...' and this unfortunate nickname followed him to university, much to the amusement of other students. 'Good God,' said one 'didn't they give you a box?' Another made paper aeroplanes and flew them in the classroom when the teacher wasn't looking.

Roman Catholics (there were not many) were excused RE lessons and religious assemblies, so one boy decided he would join them. His friends found this sudden conversion rather strange, since some of them knew he was a member of the 'Lifeboys' at Firth Park Methodist Church. But he was obviously an enterprising type, as he also describes how on Fridays he and his 'gang' would dash out first thing and pick up bottles of milk and secrete them in the wooden structure that held the water tanks in the boys' lavatories. Then, while the rest of the school was in the regular end-of-the-week assembly, he and his fellow 'converts' would be 'drinking milk and idling our time away whilst keeping an eye on the staff-room through the cracks in the woodwork'.

One rather strange confession (again, from a boy) tells of one little group who diverted themselves by picking desk-locks and forging teachers' signatures. This was not for any nefarious purpose—desks were not even opened—but the very fact of being able to do it gave them satisfaction. 'It was our proud boast that we could open any desk lock in the school.' As he says, 'Schooldays would be awfully boring without some diversion during the day'.

So here would be an appropriate place to quote a poem from a 1956 School Magazine by another boy who felt the same:

Leisure
(with apologies to W.H. Davies)

*What is this life if full of school
We have no time to play the fool?*

*No time to even pack our books
Without receiving angry looks.*

*No time to drink our milk and chatter,
Before upstairs we start to clatter.*

*No time to see the evening light,
For we're doing homework all the night.*

*No time to turn, for there's no chance
To avoid the teacher's watchful glance.*

*No time to waste: exams are here!
It's too late now to start with fear.*

*A poor life this, if full of school,
We dare not break a single rule.*

Coronation celebrations 1937

House Award

Chapter Five
Special Events and Special Care

There were always special events to break up what seemed, to the writer of *Leisure* at the end of the previous chapter, the monotony of school life. There was the Carol Service towards the end of the Autumn term and, a few days before the school broke up for the holidays, an impromptu entertainment was provided by different groups of pupils. One year some fourth-year boys produced a sketch 'Down at the Old Bull and Bush'. 'Swaying, singing with gusto, glasses in hand—cold tea, no doubt' recalls one of their friends.

Then, in 1935, the school closed for the day to mark the King and Queen's Silver Jubilee and there were games and a celebration up at the Sports Ground. A week or two later there was Empire Day to celebrate.

On January 22nd 1936 the Log Book records 'The whole school listened in to the proclamation of the new king, Edward VIII, and a few days later there was a special assembly to commemorate the reign of George V'. On May 11th of the following year, all the school went to see, and take part in, the display at Bramall Lane Cricket Ground to mark the Coronation of King George VI and Queen Elizabeth. Hundreds of pupils from different schools, each dressed in red, white or blue, marched to stirring music and everybody formed a huge Union Jack on the football pitch and the words 'Welcome to Sheffield' were written in human beings. One girl proudly remembers being part of the flag, wearing a red shirt. And afterwards? An extra week's holiday at Whitsuntide!

Later that year the schools were closed for a day, on the occasion of the new King and Queen's visit to Sheffield. Later still came the last Armistice Day Remembrance Service: by the following year another war was looming. The disruptions caused in school life by the war have already been detailed, but there was a more positive side. Apart from 'War

Weapons' Week' already mentioned, other special weeks were organised, such as 'Spitfire Week' and 'Battleship Week' to promote National Savings (and House rivalry entered into these) 'America Week' celebrated America's entry into the war in 1941.

Girls knitted balaclavas, scarves, socks and mittens for the Forces, while boys spent some of their normal Woodwork periods 'digging for victory' in Hillsborough Park—that is, helping to augment the supply of vegetables.

News of any old boys on active service was always passed on in assembly. One old boy, a former Senior Prefect, who became a pilot in the RAF, wrote 'Quite the finest inspiration I experienced while on leave was to find Marlcliffe carrying on through all these catastrophic changes with its quiet, purposeful atmosphere'. The whole of this letter was reproduced in fine calligraphy, framed and presented to the school by the Provost of Sheffield, Dr A.C.E. Jarvis, at the 1941 Speech Day.

Intermittently throughout the years various good friends of the school donated special prizes: so that, apart from the House Award for Scholarship already mentioned, there was the annual prize for 'Tidiness in Mind and Work' given by Sir Louis Smith MP at the 1939 Speech Day and, later that year, there was the first competition for the Burton Gymnastic Cup and the Pritchard Dancing Trophy. There were always, of course, subject prizes but soon, service to the school, and perseverance, were also rewarded. Indeed, by the time the school closed in 1964, 21 special prizes were listed on the Speech Day programme. Apart from these there was the Honours Board high up on the wall of the original school hall upstairs. Here, eventually, were inscribed in gold letters the names of those whose examination marks had reached Matriculation standard. Lower down, below the glazed partition walls that separated the classrooms from the hall, one could read the names of those who had gained School Certificate. However, eventually there was no more room here, so the Head ordered a special leather-bound book to be made, in which the Art Mistress each year entered, in traditional calligraphy, the names of all who had passed the School Certificate examination in five or more subjects. Any space left over on each page was enlivened by a tailpiece based on one of the subjects taught. (This book has been deposited in the City's Archives, in Shoreham Street but, unfortunately, no one seems to know what became of the Honours Board when the Intermediate School closed in 1964 and the whole building was taken over by the Junior and Infants' School.)

There were many more memorable days in the Intermediate School's forty years. In 1945 the school 'came of age' and there was a week of 21st birthday celebrations. These began with a Service in the Cathedral on Sunday, September 2nd, attended by the whole school, and on the following three days the school was open to parents and friends, both afternoon and evening; there were gymnastic and dancing displays in the hall in the

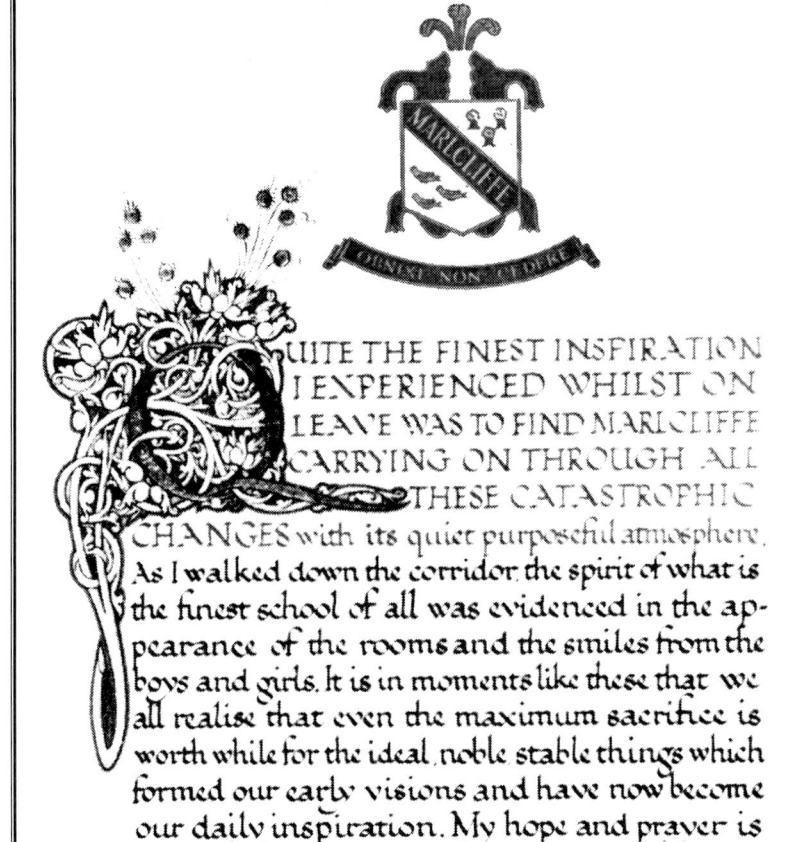

QUITE THE FINEST INSPIRATION I EXPERIENCED WHILST ON LEAVE WAS TO FIND MARLCLIFFE CARRYING ON THROUGH ALL THESE CATASTROPHIC CHANGES with its quiet purposeful atmosphere. As I walked down the corridor, the spirit of what is the finest school of all was evidenced in the appearance of the rooms and the smiles from the boys and girls. It is in moments like these that we all realise that even the maximum sacrifice is worth while for the ideal, noble stable things which formed our early visions and have now become our daily inspiration. My hope and prayer is that Marlcliffe may long continue to teach her great lessons for her sons and daughters to carry into the far corners of the world. I anticipate with eagerness the time when I shall be able to carry into the clouds the message of not only Marlcliffe but also of the whole British Empire.

OBNIXI NON CEDERE

Tom Kelly, Pilot, R.A.F. 1941. Senior Prefect 1931-1933.

Letter from Marlcliffe old boy

Booklet Produced to Celebrate Marlcliffe's 21st Birthday

MARLCLIFFE SECONDARY SCHOOL,
SHEFFIELD
– – –

August 25th, 1924—
Opening of Marlcliffe Intermediate School

December 2nd to 7th, 1945—
Coming-of-age Celebrations

– PROGRAMME –

Sunday, Dec. 2nd— 3 p.m.
   Service in the Cathedral

Monday, Dec. 3rd }
Tuesday, Dec. 4th }
Thursday, Dec. 6th }
   School open to parents and friends from
   1.30 to 5 p.m. and 6.30 to 9.30 p.m.
   Displays in Hall, 7.30 to 9.30 p.m.

Tuesday Dec. 4th— 3 to 4.30 p.m.
   Meeting of babies of past scholars, future Marlcliffians

Wednesday, Dec. 5th— 2 to 4.30 p.m.
   Birthday party for present Marlcliffians

Friday, Dec. 7th— 7.30 to 10.30 p.m.
   Birthday dinner of past Marlcliffians

MEMBERS OF STAFF

Mr W.E. Smith (Headmaster)	1924–1930
Miss N. Nuttall, B.A., (Headmistress 1930)	1924–
Mr E. Shaw, B.Sc.	1924–1930
Miss D.V. Truscott, B.A.	1924–1925
Miss S. Croydon	1924–1929
Miss I.M.E. Cox, L.L.A.	1924–1934
Miss W.B. Skinnard	1924–1936
Mr L. Reeman, B.Sc.	1924–1930
Mr H. Parkin, B.Sc.	1924–
Miss F.J. Wiles	1924–1932
Miss L.R. Todd	1925–1939
Miss M.B. Barnie, M.A.	1926–1934
Mr F.C. Reynolds, B.Sc.	1926–
Mr E.L. Parsons, B.Sc. (Econ.)	1926–1928
Mr T.W. Davis	1926–1927
Mr J.O. Beynon, B.Sc.	1927–1939
Miss D.C. Footit	1927–1933
Miss W.D. Taylor, B.Sc.	1928–1931
Mr J.R. Wassell	1929–1930
Mr E. Tomlinson, B.Sc.	1930–1940
Miss M. Renshaw, M.A.	1930–1938
Mr W. Scowcroft, B.Sc.	1930–1938
Mrs S.E. de Muschamp	1930–1932
Mr W.E. Swindell	1931–1940
Miss M.C. Coatsworth, B.A.	1931–
Mr W.E. Kelsey	1931–1935
Miss M.I. Brown	1932–1933
Mr R. Pashley, M.A.	1932–1934
Miss F. Jackson	1933–1936
Miss E.D. Bingham, M.A.	1934–1944
Mr M.A. Hawkins	1933–1935
Miss M. Varah, M.A.	1934–1936
Mr L. Egerton, B.A.	1935–1936
Miss Allum, M.A.	1934–1935

Members of Staff (continued)

Mr W.J. Hughes	1935–1938
Miss R.E. Garratt	1935–1941
Miss M.B. Watson	1936–1940
Miss M.S. Haddow	1936–1938
Miss D. Pritchard	1937–1938
Miss L. Mattocks	1938–
Miss E.L. Chandler	1938–1943
Mr R. Bainbridge, B.Sc.	1938–1940
Miss A.A. Hardie	1938–1940
Mr J. Boler	1939–1940
Mr C.F. Curtis, M.Sc.	1939–1941
Miss S. Marshall, M.A.	1939–1941
Mr H. Anderson, B.Sc.	1940–
Mr W.S. Hunt	1940–
Mr R. Harrington	1940–
Miss F. Johnstone, B.Sc.	1940–1942
Miss K.R. Scott, L.R.A.M., L.G.S.M., A.L.A.M.	1940–1942
Miss M.M. Gallimore, A.T.D.	1941–
Miss J. Lancashire, B.A.	1941–1945
Miss M. Sampson	1940–1941
Miss N. Reynolds	1942–1944
Mrs G. G. Swift, L.R.A.M., L.G.S.M	1942–
Mrs E. Scowcroft, B.Sc.	1942–
Miss J. Green	1943–
Miss G.L.S. Brooks	1944–
Miss B. Turton	1944–
Miss M.J. Gregory	1944–
Miss M. Wiley, B.A.	1945–
Mr P.G. Adams, B.A.	1945–
Miss E. Foster, L.R.A.M., A.R.C.M	1945–

SENIOR PREFECTS

Date	Girls	Boys
1924–7	Doris Stanley	Kenneth Kinns
1927	Gladys Naylor	"
1928	Peggy Appleton	Jack Redfearn
1929	Joyce Gosney	William Sharpe
1930	Laura Revitt	Gilbert Yates
1931	Alice Heaver	Arthur Roberts
1932	Minnie Wildsmith	Tom Kelly
1933	Mary Hopkinson	Joseph Wild
1934	Ida Rawson	Gilbert Gosney
1935	Joan Dean	James Clay
1936	Mary Faulkner	Harold McNair
1937	Margaret Ingledew	Paul Birch
1938	Peggy Eyre	Gordon Oldfield
1939	Joan Smith	John Hemmings
1940	Olive Walshaw	Ernest Glossop
1941	Margaret Shaw	Kenneth Dawson
1942	Barbara Coates	Eric Oldfield
1943	Dorothy Linley	Brian Dickenson
1944	Margaret Thorpe	Eric Taylor
1945	Marjorie Creasey	Brian Clarkson

HOUSE AWARD FOR ANNUAL SPORTS
THE JACKSON CUP

1926–1930	...	Swifts
1931–1934	...	Hornets
1934–1935	...	Magpies
1935–1936	...	Hornets
1936–1937	...	Bees
1937–1938	...	Rivelin
1938–1940	...	Ewden
1940–1943	...	Loxley
1943–1945	...	Ewden

HOUSE AWARD FOR SCHOLARSHIP

1937–1938	...	Ewden
1939–1940	...	Rivelin
1940–1941	...	Loxley
1942–1945	...	Ewden

SCHOOL SPORTS CHAMPIONSHIP

Date	Girls	Boys
1926	K. Bailey	K. Kinns
1927	E. Saville	,,
1928	K. Bailey	,,
1929	E. Smith	J. Malloy
1930	,,	G. Baxter
1931	A. Higginbottom	G. Hines
1932	F. Sturdy	A. Neale
1933	M. Hayes	R.A. Wilkinson
1934	,,	R. Corbett
1935	,,	G. Gosney
1936	B. Druce	J. Clay
1937	B. Hemmines	H. Gosney
1938	M. Ingledew	S. Else
1939	D. Jubb	N. McNair
1940	K. Wilson	P. Savage
1941	M. Wells & J. Barratt	E. Glossop
1942	D. Raymonde	E. Oldfield
1943	J. Radley	,,
1944	D. Crofts	B. Shepherd
1945	,,	R. Hall

SCHOOL SOCIETIES

WIRELESS & SCIENTIFIC SOCIETY
RAMBLERS' SOCIETY
DRAMATIC SOCIETY
KNITTING CIRCLE
HANDICRAFT GUILD
FOLK DANCING SOCIETY
MODERN DANCING SOCIETY
FRENCH CIRCLE

SCHOOL PLAYS

1928	"The Rivals"	R.P. Sheridan
1929	'She Stoops to Conquer"	O. Goldsmith
1930	"Quality Street"	J.M. Barrie
1931	"The Admirable Crichton"	J. M. Barrie
1932	"The Romantic Age"	A.A. Milne
	"Spreading the News"	Lady Gregory
1933	"Inheritors"	Susan Glaspell
1934	"The Aristocrat"	Louis N. Parker
1935	"The Grand Cham's Diamond"	A. Monkhouse
	"Campbell of Kilmhor"	J.A. Ferguson
	"The Invisible Duke"	F. Slayden-Smith
1936	"The Late Christopher Bean"	Emlyn Williams
1937	"Lady Precious Stream"	I.S. Hsiung
1938	"Toad of Toad Hall"	A.A. Milne
1939	"Viceroy Sarah"	N. Ginsburg
1941	"Pride & Prejudice"	H. Jerome
1942	"Gallows Glorious"	R. Gow
1943	"The Lady with a Lamp"	R. Berkeley
1944	"Saint Joan"	G.B. Shaw
1945	"Through the Crack"	Algernon Blackwood

SCHOOL EXCURSIONS

Paris:
Parties of Marlcliffians spent Easter Week in Paris, in 1927, 1928, 1929, 1930, 1931, and 1938.

Bridlington:
At the end of the School Certificate Examination, from 1928 to 1933, Fourth Year scholars spent a day at Bridlington.

Ramblers Society:
In addition to rambles, visits to local places of interest and to works, annual outings to:-

1928	York	1934	York
1929	Lincoln	1935	London
1930	York	1936	Edinburgh
1931	York	1937	Stratford-on-Avon
1932	Lincoln	1938	London
1933	Liverpool	1939	Edinburgh or Liverpool & Chester

SPECIAL PRIZES

Many special prizes have been given by friends of Marlcliffe. The following list is of prizes given for five years or more:-

French
Given by Ald. H.W. Jackson, LL.B. ... 1928–45
Geography
Given by A.A. Brown, Esq. ... 1928–45
English Essay
E.W. Smith, Esq. ... 1928–38

Special Prizes (continued)
English Literature
Given by Mrs H.W. Jackson ... 1930–45
History
Given by Coun. G.E. Marlow, J.P. ... 1935–45
Mathematics
Given by W.W. Armitage, Esq. ... 1930–45
Domestic Science
Given by Miss F.J. Wiles ... 1937–45
Handwriting
Given by H.S. Newton, Esq., M.A. ... 1932–41
Best Marlcliffian
Given by Mrs R.E. Sopwith ... 1934–49
Scripture
Given by Ald. H.E. Bridgwater, J.P. ... 1935–45
Perseverance
Given by Ald. Mrs A.E. Longden, J.P. ... 1939–45
Best Marlcliffian Boy
Given by R.E. Sopwith, Esq., B.A., B.Com. 1940–45
Best Marlcliffian Girl
Given by Mrs R.E. Sopwith ... 1940–45
Service to the School
Given by Mrs W.M. Watkins ... 1940–45
Tidiness in Mind and Work
Given by Lady Smith ... 1940–45
English Essay
Given by F. Carr, Esq. ... 1940–45
Senior Knitting
Given by Miss M. Renshaw, M.A ... 1940-45

TROPHIES

Cup for Annual Sports		
Presented by Ald. H.W. Jackson, LL.B. …		1926
Cup for Netball		
Presented by Miss Croydon … …		1930
Cup for Stoolball		
Presented by Miss Cox … …		1934
Dancing Trophy		
Presented by Miss Pritchard … …		1939
Physical Training Cup		
Presented by J. Burton, Esq. … …		1939
House Award for Scholarship		
Presented by Miss Nuttall, B.A. … …		1937

SPEECH DAY GUESTS OF HONOUR

Aldermann E.G. Rowlinson, J.P.
The First Lord of the Admiralty, Rt. Hon. A.V. Alexander, M.P.
The Lord Mayor of Sheffield, Alderman H.W. Jackson, LL.B.
The Lord Mayor of Sheffield, Alderman T.H. Watkins
Miss E.M. Maxfield, J.P.
The Lord Bishop of Sheffield, Dr. L.H. Burrows
The Vice-Chancellor of the University of Sheffield, Dr A.W. Pickard-Cambridge, M.A., F.B.A.
Lady Mabel Smith
The Lord Mayor of Sheffield, Councillor Mrs. A.E. Longden, J.P.
Sir Percival Sharp, LL.D., B.Sc.
Sir Louis Smith, M.P.
The Lord Mayor of Sheffield, Alderman J.A. Longden, J.P.
The Provost of Sheffield, Dr A.C.E. Jarvis, C.B., C.M.G., M.C.
His Honour Judge R.C. Essenhigh
The Lord Mayor of Sheffield, Councillor H.E. Bridgwater, J.P.
Pro-Chancellor of the University of Sheffield, Sir Samuel Osborn, LL.D., J.P.
President of the Association of Education Com‑ mittees, Alderman H.W. Jackson, LL.B.
....

Chairman at every Speech Day from 1932 to 1944 Alderman H.W. Jackson, LL.B.

FURTHER FACTS AND FIGURES

In the twenty-one years since August 25th, 1924, 2803 scholars admitted.

The percentage of successes of scholars who stayed four years to take the School Certificate Examination, from 1928 to 1945 is 83.4. The highest percentage in any year is 94.4. The highest individual result is eight distinctions and one credit.

Except that no play was produced in 1940, owing to Home Service conditions, every year, from 1928 to 1945, a Speech Day, a Sports Day, and a School Play.

A School Magazine was published at least twice annually from 1924 to 1939. All magazines from 1933 to 1939 were printed by Marlcliffians, and from 1934 to 1939 had original illustrations and cover designs.

School Houses from 1924 to 1936 were Bees, Hornets, Magpies, Swifts. From 1936. Ewden, Loxley, Rivelin.

Marlcliffe was one of the first schools to introduce wireless in 1924.

A new building was opened in 1937.

National Savings total £5930.

In 1944 and 1945 admission of classes of 13-plus scholars, with a view to becoming teachers, in addition to the usual 120 annual admission of 11-plus scholars.

Special Events and Special Care

evening. On one day there was what the programme described as a 'Meeting of babies of past scholars, future Marlcliffians': this caused very welcome disruption of lessons as mothers carried their children from classroom to classroom, re-living old memories. The following afternoon was given over to fun and a birthday tea for the present pupils and then, next evening, the old scholars met for a 'Birthday Dinner'. The printed programme for these events lists all the staff from 1924 onwards, all the Senior Prefects, Sports Champions, sports trophies and special prizes, all the school societies, plays, school excursions and, finally, the guests of honour at Speech Days. It also records the fact that Alderman (later Sir) Harold Jackson had been Chairman at every Speech Day from 1932 to 1944.

Mention of Alderman Jackson brings to mind another less happy occasion. In 1959 Lady Jackson died, and it is indicative of her feeling for the school that she had expressed a wish that a guard of honour of Marlcliffe prefects should accompany her coffin at the funeral. It was winter-time and the girl prefects thought that Miss Nuttall might allow them to wear stockings, instead of the regulation white ankle socks, secretly hoping that 'if this were allowed, maybe we would rid ourselves of the hated ankle socks permanently and maintain our dignity as fashionable young women'. Their request was refused but 'full of our own importance and certain that we were right, and with enthusiastic support from the boys, we walked out of school and refused to do our duties'. Anarchy! But soon Miss Nuttall called them into her office and 'listened to our concerns about possible chills in such unpleasant weather, our wish to be allowed to dress as pupils in other schools were allowed to, and finally our sincere wish to appear smartly dressed for this important event'. At first this seemed to work, Miss Nuttall agreed that, in view of the cold, stockings would be better and she 'opened a drawer and pulled out a pair, but told us that we could only wear stockings of the type she held up—thick, knitted wool ones'. (They went to the funeral in ankle socks.)

Pupils were involved with the teachers during lessons, societies, outings, sports; but there were other more personal encounters between staff and pupils which are very revealing. One girl remembers breaking her ankle; she was taken to hospital, of course, but afterwards the Senior Master took her home and bought her chocolates! Another came out of hospital to find that her father had deserted the family. She became quite unruly but, when the Head became aware of the situation, she sent for the girl and impressed on her that she should think 'I must show everyone that I can succeed in spite of my difficulties, not fail because of them'. (Miss Nuttall was well placed to give this advice, as she herself gained her Honours Degree the hard way, studying at evening classes.) Also, this girl once had a ten shilling note, given by her mother to pay a bill, taken from her coat pocket. She was standing panic-stricken after the discovery when one of the masters stopped to ask her what was wrong. When she told him, he gave her ten shillings but said she must save up until she could pay him back by doing odd jobs, running errands and going without some of her pocket money. When she eventually came to repay him he wouldn't take the money but told her to use it to start a savings account, gently remarking 'for most people things don't come easily and one should take care of what one has'.

One boy gratefully remembers the teacher who helped him to cope with taking a School Certificate examination on the very day of his mother's funeral, and took him home by taxi afterwards. A girl on a similar occasion remembers how comforting one teacher was—a teacher whom she'd previously thought of as rather severe.

Another girl was caught passing round, amongst her giggling friends, a filthy verse but, when the teacher asked her what she really thought about it, she said 'horrible!' This was the cue for the teacher to say that, as she knew, God created the first man but after that he passed on to us the act of creation and, if a man and woman truly loved each other, such an act was a wonderful experience. As another girl expresses it: 'The staff at Marlcliffe maybe didn't use the term Pastoral Care but they were as good at it as any present-day teachers'.

So far, no individual teachers have been named, except for the first Headmaster, Mr Smith; and his successor, Miss Nuttall; but, as I mentioned earlier, exceptions must be made for the long-serving Senior Master and Senior Mistress.

Mr F.C. Reynolds BSc came to the school in 1926 and stayed until his retirement. He taught Algebra and Science to the Junior forms and Scripture to the Seniors. 'Stern but well-liked', 'a great teacher, one of the very best', 'the mainstay of the organisation', 'a regular good man.' He was a firm supporter of the Old Marlcliffians' Association (of which more later) being first the Treasurer, then Secretary for several years, and eventually President. In 1937 the OMA Minute Book records him as pleading for the members to bring in other old scholars—'the Marlcliffians in outer darkness'. Mr Reynolds retired in 1960 and died ten years later.

Miss M.C. Coatsworth BA came to the school in 1931 and stayed until its closure in 1964. Her initials were MCC—very appropriate for someone as keen on sport as she was—but no one dare use her first name of Martha for she hated it. (Indeed, in those far-off days, even members of staff didn't call one another by their Christian names.) She taught History to the Seniors and, according to one boy, 'warned that in case of bad behaviour there would be wars and rumours of wars, but she was very kind'. On at least one occasion, she invited a group of pupils to tea in her flat. She, too, supported the various activities of the Old Marlcliffians—as Miss Nuttall said, she was a most enthusiastic member,

Special Events and Special Care 53

and one couldn't imagine an OMA meeting without her. Even after her retirement in 1970, when she returned to her native North Yorkshire, she still came back to Sheffield for the annual reunion. Sadly, by 1994 deteriorating health made this no longer possible, but she wrote a very moving letter to her old pupils. She died the following year.

1951
Mr Booth, Mr Goddard, Mr Outram, Mr Walton
Mrs Scowcroft, Miss Whitehead, Miss Saunders, Miss Littlewood, Miss Underdown, Miss Swift,
Mr Thompson, Miss Chellingworth
Mr Anderson, Mr Parkin, Miss Mattocks, Mr Reynolds, Miss Nuttall, Miss Coatsworth, Mr Hunt,
Mrs Bramhill, Mr Harrington

October 1996

Dear Old Marcliffians,

This is being written for the younger members of you so that they know not only how the school came to exist, but also the factors that made Marlcliffe what all of us, young or old, believe it to have been: 'The Best School of All'

Since, however, to many of the older members, all or part of this is no news, I shall refer to everyone as 'You' throughout. You are going to find this very different from my previous unprepared ramblings about unrelated, nostalgic incidents I valued from my own young days at Marlcliffe.

First of all, Marlcliffe would never have existed had it not been for Alderman, later Sir, Harold Jackson. He thought there were not enough Grammar School places but more could be provided 'On The Cheap' by four new Intermediate Schools. In these days of uniform pay for teachers, this would have been impossible. In those days fortunately for you and your chance of advanced education this was not the case. Salaries varied not only from area to area but from school to school according to size and type.

The school once founded, owed its successful development to three groups. These worked closely together under very difficult conditions from those enjoyed by you at a later date.

Group I The Scholars—(a) particularly the founder members who laid the basis of its standards (b) those during the 'Thirties' who built on that foundation.

Group II The Staff—(a) Again the founder members who began the societies (b) those during the 'Thirties" who carried on the good work.

Group III The Parents who supported every activity of the growing school e.g. Armistice Day Service, School Play, Speech Day, Sports Day, Open Days etc. even to knitting socks, scarves and balaclavas to be sent to Marcliffians with the armed forces when their unit could be identified.

To show the different conditions referred to before, I'll take one example. There were no games in school hours. Staff and scholars went on Saturday morning to Myers Grove Lane, whilst the parents faced the dilemma of whether they could afford to allow their children to go. There were so many unemployed that the few coppers a child could earn by working, would greatly add to the family budget.

At the beginning of the war (1939) the last two periods of one afternoon a week were given to games. The parents had no decision to make. The scholars set off at the beginning of playtime to walk in formation to Myers Grove Lane accompanied by the staff. The three groups worked closely together as a team and like all teams needed a Captain. That captain was of course Miss Nuttall. She made clear to Marlcliffians, scholars, staff and parents what she wanted.

Fundamentally all worked together for the good of Marlcliffe, essentially loyal to each other and the school. Yes, you were made to work hard, suffer exams in all subjects, twice a year, Xmas and Midsummer. Worse was to follow, the results were published to the school at large so you were shamed into doing better. Yes, you were made to obey orders or you were disciplined. This took three forms (1) lines (2) detention (3) corporal punishment. The last alternative never applied to girls nor women staff. Neither of these out of date methods of examinations or discipline seem to have done any of you much harm!

You were encouraged (a) to work with one another in all age groups in House competitions, (b) to compete enthusiastically but fairly with other Schools, (c) to realise that you could expect no right without responsibility, every privilege carried its own obligation.

Those of you who suffered the disadvantages of those pre-war years, had one outstanding advantage. The school and staff were small, everyone knew everyone else. We were a compact unit and realised that bricks and mortar do not make a school. It is made by the spirit of one-ness and friendliness inside it.

This was made abundantly clear to those of you who returned to wish me a 'happy retirement' in 1970. The buildings had improved, the amenities had improved but the Spirit had gone. No shields, no cups and no school motto, in fact 'our' school was there no more.

After forming the school as a united family, Miss Nuttall turned her attention to forming your ideas and characters as individuals. This was accomplished by the dedication of her life to the service of her God and the carrying out of His laws. These in the main are shown in the commandments, particularly in the words of Jesus.

'Thou shalt love the Lord, thy God with all thy heart and with all thy Soul and with all thy Mind and with all thy Strength. This is the first great commandment and the second is like unto it.'

'Thou shalt love thy Neighbour as thyself'.

You will see that in both cases the dominant word is 'Love'. If you carry out these two to the best of your ability, the other eight become almost irrelevant. I should like to end this part of my letter with a quotation from Sir Henry Newbolt's poetry. I am a great admirer of his work for the very reasons that the present generation (which no doubt includes many of you) considers him out of date. My admiration stems from the fact that his poetry not only rhymes and has rhythm, but he also insists on recognising his debts and paying honour to the people and institutions who helped and influenced him in his youth.

> We'll honour yet the school we knew,
> The best school of all;
> We'll honour yet the rule we knew,
> Till the last bell call.
> For, working days or holidays,
> And glad or melancholy days,
> They were great days and jolly days
> At the best school of all.

OBNIXI NON CEDERE

Now comes the more difficult part of my letter. I cannot express what Marlcliffe gave to me even from the first day I entered its doors. However much it cost I could never repay the debt. You all understand that because you are all members of the same close knit, loving family created by our three groups and Captain.

I want to say thank you to those of you who have kept me in that same family group, not only when we were at Marlcliffe nor when some of us had departed for pastures new, but also when I retired. In a very short time after that I was compelled to retire to my native North Riding and North Yorks Moors. This could have cut me off from the family. That it did not do so was due entirely to many of you.

I was kept up to date by letters, visits and unexpected treats from other members of the family. e.g.. Some on a visit North on business made a detour on the way back to call; others en route to or from holiday came out of their way to visit me. Some came up for the day. Some came to stay. I was therefore in close contact with the family, in spite of the loss of Staff colleagues of my early, home service and wartime years at Marlcliffe when the reunions started. In fact that is how I heard of them in the first place. I am not going to specify what I owe to many of you for the period of their existence. I just want to say 'Thanks' to all for what you have done to make my participation in and my enjoyment of them possible. I could not put on paper all the kindnesses I have received from each and every one of you without omitting someone. Therefore the thanks must be general because you have all helped in some way. Many of you may think anything you have done has been too small to matter. I assure you that all the kindnesses have been appreciated.

When you have read this, you will know that in body, I have not been with you this year. In spirit I have been with you throughout. I hope you sing all the verses of the School Song. Every verse brings memories of each of you to my mind. You'll know which verse refers to you!

In conclusion 'Goodbye' to those of you I shall not see again. I hope some of you may pay me a visit.

Bless you! My love to you all,
Please remember me in your prayers,

Colleen Coatsworth

1961
Mr Parkin, Mr Smith, Captain Outram, Mr Briggs, Mr Crookes, Mr Barnby
Miss Coyle, Mrs Haley, Miss Smith, Miss Jackson, Mr Littlewood, Mrs Thomson, Mrs Keen, Mrs Cooper
Miss Whitehead, Mr Walton, Mrs Bramhill, Mr Parkin, Miss Nuttall, Miss Coatsworth,
Mr Anderson, Miss Chellingworth, Mr Harrington

Chapter Six
The Old Marlcliffians' Association

The last verse of the school song runs thus:

> *Throughout the years Marlcliffians, when days at school are o'er,*
> *The spirit that inspires us shall be to all revealed;*
> *For those with whom we labour shall know for evermore*
> *Marlcliffians, yea, Marlcliffians, have hearts set not to yield.*

One thing that happened 'when days at school are o'er' was the founding of the Old Marlcliffians' Association. Even as early as 1928, some of the first entrants who were leaving decided that they must keep in touch, and soon sports activities were started, including matches against present scholars. The first OMA Christmas Dinner was a small-scale affair, and took place in the wooden building which then served as the School Hall—and it was the caretaker who cooked the meal!

By 1932, rambles, dances and what were called 'charabanc excursions' were added, and also a Bonfire Night party—with 'parkin, roast potatoes, butter and tea!' A hundred former pupils attended the dinner that year.

After that there were monthly meetings of one sort or another until the war broke out in 1939.

Two Minute Books of the Society, covering the years 1932–64 have survived and it is worth recording that already, at the 1932 Annual General Meeting, 118 members were present and, as the Minute Book records, the President spoke of the joy of renewing old friendships. Four resolutions were proposed and passed:

> That, as the OMA is a mixed association, the President should be alternately a lady or gentleman.
>
> That wine should be provided for the guests at the Annual Dinner.
>
> That the Head of the School be always an ex-officio member of the Committee.

and

> That former pupils should be able to become life members for 10 shillings.

This same year a former teacher offered an 'Old Marlcliffian Snap Album'—one wonders if this has survived and, if so, where is it now?

Various prominent citizens were invited as guests to the Annual Dinner which must have been quite a lengthy affair to judge from the programme for 1933:

1. Toast—the King
2. Presentation to Mrs Pennington[1]
3. Pianoforte solo
4. Toast—the School
5. Song
6. Toast—the Association
7. Entertainer
8. Toast—our Guests
9. Song
10. The School Song
11. Auld Lang Syne

By the next year, whist drives and swimming parties at Glossop Road Baths had been added to the activities but, was the Association perhaps becoming a little too ambitious? At the AGM that year the Treasurer reported on 'the grave financial state of the Association'— there was a debit balance of 1s 9d! (roughly 10p). Next year lemonade was to be provided at the dinner but still 'a suitable bottle of wine for the guests at the top table'.

Soon it was decided that scholars in their last year at school could become members and, by 1937, things were looking up—55 members at the AGM and 106 at the dinner, and cash in hand was £6 18s 0d.

Activities continued until the summer of 1939 but there was no Annual Dinner that year and no more evening meetings. By 1946, after the war, the society was back to monthly fixtures and a 'Dramatic Night' was included. This led to the formation of an old pupils' Dramatic Society but there is no detail of its activities in the first Minute Book.

---

1. A former member of staff who had left on marriage

The Old Marlcliffians' Association

Old Marlcliffians' production of 'Relative Values' 1954

An important event in 1951 was the presentation to the school by the Association of a carved oak table and chair, made by Robert Thompson of Kilburn, whose trademark of a carved mouse was always to be found on his work. This was a gesture by the old scholars to mark the 21st birthday of their own Association. Henceforth the table and chair were always on the platform in the school hall.

Meanwhile the OMA Dramatic Society continued with annual productions although, in 1955, the Secretary was appealing for more acting and non-acting members. The next year the Association's Secretary reported that, on the whole, the year's activities had been poorly supported. Later reports at committee meetings give the same picture but one special event in 1962 was very different: this was the year of Miss Nuttall's retirement, after 38 years at Marlcliffe, 32 of them as Headmistress. At a special meeting the Old Marlcliffians' Association made a presentation of a bookcase, and very many old pupils turned up to shake Miss Nuttall's hand and wish her well. (One student at school then remembers that, after her last school assembly, Miss Nuttall herself shook every pupil by the hand as they filed out.)

As a résumé of her life in teaching, one cannot do better than quote the interview of a *Sheffield Telegraph* reporter on July 13th 1962:

One Woman's World: By Christine Cartwright

'School Leaver'—After 45 Years' Service

The first thing you notice is a shock of silvery hair, then the laugh, a deep infectious chuckle, and finally the hands—square, capable, with splayed fingers constantly moving to stab home an important point in the conversation.

Conversing is something Miss Nellie Nuttall does well, switching rapidly from her belief in the present-day teenager to what it was like in Grenoside 60 years ago when she was a small girl.

In exactly two weeks she retires from a teaching career that began 45 years ago, with 38 of those years at the same school—Marlcliffe Secondary—opened as an Intermediate School in 1924.

Miss Nuttall was on the original staff as English Mistress. Six years later she became Headmistress, watching succeeding generations of Marlcliffians pass through the school, and out into the adult world.

Bookcases

Next Friday two of the many presentations that are being made to mark her retirement will be held. Old scholars—two are coming from Middlesex and one from Hertfordshire—are giving her bookcases 'among other things' and the past and present staff are providing furniture for a complete kitchen.

When Miss Nuttall arrived at Marlcliffe there were 120 pupils, 60 boys and 60 girls. The type of school was a new venture for Sheffield, but the Headmaster, Mr Walter Smith, was backed up by a staff determined to meet the challenge of bridging the gap between grammar schools and the 'senior' schools of that day.

With his backing, Miss Nuttall set about building up a school tradition. She wrote the school song, started a magazine (still printed on the premises), pioneered the dramatic and rambling societies, and eventually started school visits to the Continent.

'The first one, which must have been about 1927, cost us £5' she said. 'We kept them up until the adverse exchange rate in the 1930s, and later the war made us stop temporarily.'

Hazards

The war was only one of the hazards that faced the school during Miss Nuttall's leadership. She watched it through the trade depression of the 1920s—'in those days pupils weren't asked to sign an agreement that they would stay their full course, so we lost many when they became old enough to take home 5s'; the General Strike; the 1930s financial crisis, and now 'The Bulge'.

'Today's parents are very much more aware of the need for education' she said, 'and the children themselves are wonderful, confident, and happy, and willing to help other people.'

'When I first became a teacher,' (she is a BA of London University) 'many of the pranks that today pass as juvenile delinquency would be dealt with by the policeman on the spot, and never be taken to the courts.'

In general education, she feels that the range of subjects taught has widened considerably, while intensive training in the three Rs has lessened.

Intrigued

But the one point about 45 years in the teaching profession that intrigued me was how Miss Nuttall managed to get to know all the thousands of children by name.

'Ah,' she smiled, 'one knows that this is young Michael because no one has ever climbed stairs quite so noisily before, or that was Jane, plaits and intense blue eyes, and top in English. Some little characteristic makes them all individual, and all of them worth knowing.'

She thought for a few moments, then summed up her entire career in one remark.

'You know,' she said, 'when they made me Headmistress, they lost a teacher.'

Miss Nuttall's Retirement   6th April 1962

Rowley Nuttall (brother), Mr Parkin, Miss Nuttall, Mr Reynolds, Miss Coatsworth

Mrs Keen with Domestic Science Pupils

But no, Marlcliffe didn't lose a teacher: teaching is more than sitting in front of a class; Miss Nuttall's whole attitude was an education to those under her care. Happily, her sterling contribution to education in Sheffield was recognised by an invitation to the Buckingham Palace Garden Party that year. Finally—and what a nice touch!—a fuchsia has been named after her.

For the next two years, Marlcliffe carried on under the acting headship of Mr H. Parkin, BSc, who had taught there since 1924. But, in the summer of 1964, the school that had served Sheffield so well for 40 years closed. The idea of 'selection' at the age of 11 was no longer acceptable, so the Marlcliffe pupils and staff joined the Secondary Modern School on the Parson Cross estate and the whole school became Chaucer Comprehensive where pupils of all abilities were taught.

Later that year an Extraordinary General Meeting of the Old Marlcliffians' Association was held to discuss future plans, and it was decided by a two-thirds majority to carry on with the Association and at least have an Annual Dinner. However, interest in the other activities waned—the Dramatic section had already closed—and after one more Annual Dinner it was obvious that there was insufficient support to keep this going, so, like the school itself, the OMA quietly disappeared.

Nevertheless, there were many who regretted this and kept in touch amongst themselves and, over 20 years later, there were two stalwarts who, true to their old school motto Obnixi non Cedere (determined not to yield) decided to try to revive the Association.

In 1988 a letter was sent to the Star suggesting a meeting of former pupils and about 70 turned up. It was then decided to hold a more informal annual lunch—without the guests and toasts and entertainment of the dinners of the past—and this idea obviously went down well for the following year over 140 met at the lunch. Sometimes there were more than this, and even in 1996 over a hundred. It was on this occasion that the idea of compiling a book of memories of the old school was mooted and received enthusiastic support. Sadly, there were no members of staff left who had known the school since its earliest days; so the task of writing the book fell to one who had taught there for 23 years.

Questionnaires were given out to those present to fill in, and more former pupils were contacted by word of mouth, letter or telephone. It is all these Old Marlcliffians who have made this little book possible. Nearly all of them describe the members of staff of their day, but one appreciation of the Head, and of the school generally, comes from a girl who became a Headmistress herself; it seems a particularly appropriate ending to this book of memories:

The Old Marlcliffians' Association

Miss Nuttall, a small but fearsome lady, a strict disciplinarian, albeit with a twinkle in her eye. Marlcliffe provided an environment in which I personally felt valued. Criticism was always constructive, never harsh. Understanding, encouragement, friendly discipline constituted the ethos of Marlcliffe. We worked hard, we liked the people who taught us and respected their attitude. I am eternally grateful for the education which provided the basis for my entering a career which gave me so much joy.

Miss Nuttall